Cross Stitch Patterns

Revised Edition

Edited by Thelma M. Nye

Balkans	Ida-Merete Erlandsen
Ancient China	Antonette Prip-Møller
Denmark	Else Johnsen
Ancient Peru	Ellen Jessen

 VAN NOSTRAND REINHOLD COMPANY
New York   Cincinnati   Toronto   London   Melbourne

Van Nostrand Reinhold Company Regional Offices:
New York   Cincinnati   Chicago   Millbrae   Dallas

Van Nostrand Reinhold Company International Offices:
London   Toronto   Melbourne

First published in the United States of America 1970
Library of Congress Catalog Card Number 72-9572
ISBN 0-442-25998-0
Printed and bound in Denmark by
S.L. Møllers, Bogtrykkeri, Copenhagen
Revised edition published in 1973 by
Van Nostrand Reinhold Company
A Division of Litton Educational Publishing, Inc.
450 West 33rd Street, New York, N.Y. 10001

16   15   14   13   12   11   10   9   8   7   6   5   4   3   2   1

2

INTRODUCTION

Working in cross stitch gives great enjoyment to embroiderers of all ages and abilities. Here is a book containing over a hundred charts of motifs and patterns all of which can be worked in the normal cross stitch. These can be interpreted in countless ways and on materials of varying weaves, and in threads of varying thicknesses, thus producing different effects. Symbols show possible variations of colour and stitch within the pattern but these are merely suggestions and the individual embroiderer may well have other ideas. The following diagrams show clearly the formation of cross stitch, together with variations with which experiment should be encouraged.

CROSS STITCH
This is worked on a fabric of which the threads can be counted.

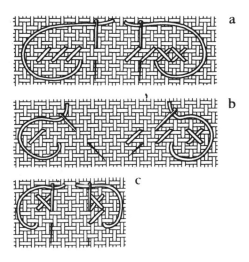

(a) Horizontal rows Work all the under stitches first, from left to right, then the over stitches the reverse way. The stitches on the wrong side are vertical.

(b) Horizontal rows with spacing Work all the under stitches from the

left, the over stitches from the right. The wrong side stitches form crosses.

(c) Vertical rows Work each cross individually, the under stitch first from the left, the over stitch from the right. All the stitches on the wrong side are vertical.

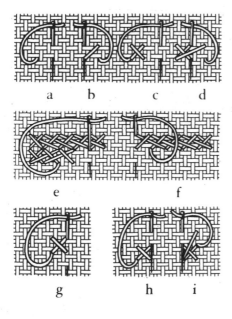

a   b   c   d

e   f

g   h   i

(a) Bring the needle up in the bottom left-hand corner and take an oblique stitch to the right.

(b) Make an oblique stitch back.

(c) Take an oblique stitch of double length further to the right.

(d) Make an oblique stitch back.

(e) Complete the row, finishing with a cross stitch.

(f) Work the next row in the same manner but with the movements reversed.

(g) Shows a single stitch.

(h-i) Show the stitch worked vertically, as it might be used for long single rows. Bring the needle up on the left, work an oblique stitch to the right, an oblique stitch to the left, an oblique stitch of double length upwards to the right and an oblique stitch to the left.

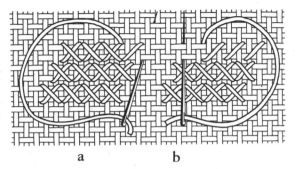

a   b

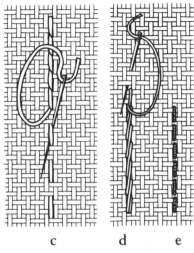

c d e

STAGGERED CROSS STITCH

Not only the ordinary type of cross stitch is used, in which the individual stitches lie directly underneath each other, but frequently the type of cross stitch known as *staggered* is used. With this stitch, it is often possible to achieve a simpler pattern and save on the number of stitches; it is of special value in those places where it is necessary to sew narrow, sloping stripes very close to each other. The effect of an expanse of staggered cross stitch is different from the effect of the type in which the stitches lie directly underneath each other.

(a) The first row is worked as usual; the next row has an uneven number of threads to one side so that the needle does not come to pierce the old holes of the row above, but the holes lying in between.

(b) The third row has an uneven number of threads to the side in relation to the second row, and the stitches in the third row come to lie directly over the stitches in the first row, and so on.

Sometimes *double running stitches,* or Holbein stitches, are used for outlining a motif in cross stitch or for separating colors inside a motif.

(c) The row of stitches is sewn in two steps. The stitches made the second time surface where those made the first time went to the reverse, and vice versa.

STEM STITCH

The stem stitch is used for both outlining and filling in. The ordinary stem stitch is worked in a straight line upward or to the right over four threads of the ground fabric and back under two. The stitches will overlap on the front, so that there will be a double row of thread. The thread is kept to the right of or below the needle. The needle with the embroidery thread picks up two threads of the linen in each stitch. When used for filling in, the lines of stem stitch should be made parallel and quite near to each other.

When the motifs have long straight or sloping jagged stripes, it is often an advantage to sew the stripes first and put on the jags afterward. When the motif itself is finished, the background should be completely filled in as far as possible, with stem stitch sewn in long, straight lines. The embroidery thread passes on the reverse of the linen when these lines of background stitches cross the stripes of the motif.

If the lines of the motif form an angle, the sewing is continued over the angle, thus smoothing out the

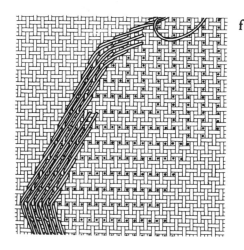

f

6

angular nature of the design.

(d) stem stitch shown from the right side of the fabric

(e) stem stitch shown from the reverse side of the fabric

(f) detail from the sewing of angles in stem stitch. Both a simple and a more complicated angle are shown

UPRIGHT STITCHES

Stripes can be sewn in a number of different stitches. Stem stitches are used for vertical stripes and for filling in. Upright *gobelin stitches* may be used for horizontal stripes. Upright *Florentine stitches* may be used for sloping stripes. These gobelin and Florentine stitches are usually made in double groups, but instead of sewing them twice, they can be sewn only once with a double thread.

(g) Upright gobelin stitches are made over two threads

(h) Upright Florentine stitches are worked over four horizontal threads, each stitch starting two threads above the last. The short horizontal rows shown here were added later.

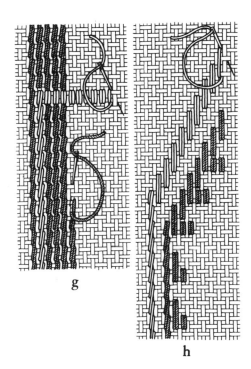

g

h

7

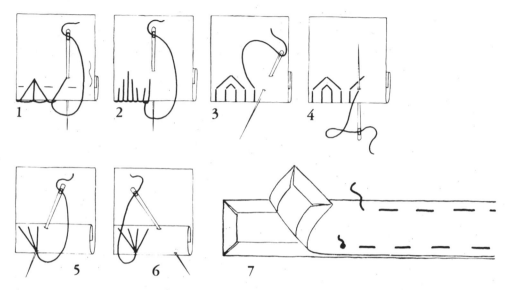

1   2   3   4

5   6   7

Hems Many pieces of work are finished off with a hem turned towards the wrong side of the material but an attractive effect can be achieved by turning it to the right side instead. The hem can be finished off with scallop stitches, as in A, B and C, or with various kinds of overcast stitches as in D, E, F and G.

The stitches can be varied in an infinite number of ways.

Hems with scallop stitching Turn the hem downwards and start stitching from the left (figures 1 and 2) with vertical stitches, keeping the loose thread under the needle.

Hems with overcast stitches Turn the hem downwards and start stitching from the left. (Figures 3 and 4).

Where the stitches are to be at an angle it will often be found necessary to pass the needle through the material right out to the edge. (Figures 5 and 6).

Fig H shows an apron-ribbon on a child's apron; it has been made out of

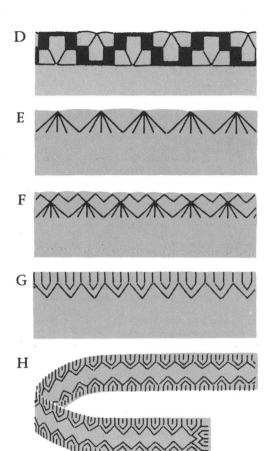

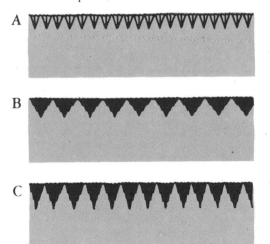

two strips of material whose edges have been turned in towards each other, tacked together and sewn with stitches. (Figure 7).

Note To ensure the correct position the pattern should be calculated by counting from the centre. Where necessary, this has been indicated by a small arrow. In the case of borders which it has been necessary to divide into two rows, the point of juncture has been indicated by a large arrow. The circular patterns covering four pages are joined just beyond the edges and positioned by counting from the centre.

COLOR CODES
The Balkans: Color Codes to DMC
Thread Numbers in the Patterns

	899	deep pink
	444	yellow
	838	brown
	3347	pale green
	799	pale blue
	797	blue
	823	dark blue
	936	dark green
		white
	606	red
	597	pale bluish green
	3687	red violet
	310	black
	904	green
	742	warm yellow
	304	dark red
	350	coral red
	911	deep green
	553	violet
	806	dark turquoise
	435	pale brown
	315	deep old rose
	931	blue gray
	307	lemon yellow
	605	pale red
	740	pale orange
	915	dark red
	745	pale yellow
	701	grass green

	946	deep orange

Page 17

	310	black
	606	red
	444	yellow

Page 18

above

	3347	pale green
	304	dark red
	350	coral red

below

	904	green
	304	dark red
	350	coral red

Page 19

	838	brown
	606	red

Page 20

above

	797	blue
	799	pale blue
	606	red

below

	606	red
	838	brown

Page 21

	606	red
	310	black

Page 22

	838	brown
	350	coral red

Page 23

above

	936	dark green
	444	yellow

below

	838	brown (single-ply)
	899	deep pink

Page 24

	310	black
	606	red

Page 35

	310	black
	899	deep pink

Page 39

above

	310	black (single-ply)

below

	310	black
	350	coral red

Page 40

	310	black (single-ply)

Page 45

	838	brown

Page 46

	823	dark blue
	931	blue gray

Denmark: Color Codes to the Patterns

- dull yellow
- ochre
- dull reddish orange
- light brick red
- dull bluish red
- dark bluish red
- dark brown
- gray
- navy blue
- lavender
- dull bluish green
- dark green
- black
- axis of symmetrical design

Ancient Peru: Color Codes to DMC Thread Numbers in the Patterns

Page 102*

	336	dark blue
	437	warm yellow
	731	olive

Page 103

	312	blue
	347	red
	367	green

Pages 104-105*

	367	green
	791	dark blue
	437	warm yellow

Page 106*

	437	warm yellow
	336	dark blue
	367	green

Page 107

	437	yellow
	347	red
	501	dark green

Page 108*

		ecru
	744	yellow
	402	pale orange
	791	dark blue
	300	brown
	501	dark green

Page 109

		white
	437	warm yellow
	433	brown
	642	gray
	761	rose pink
	347	red
	793	pale blue
	791	dark blue
	937	green

Page 110

		white
	437	warm yellow
	920	terra-cotta
	320	green
	794	pale blue
	938	dark brown
	644	pale gray
	437	warm yellow
	931	pale blue
	801	brown
	356	pale red
	502	green
		white
	437	warm yellow
	356	pale red
	320	green
	931	blue

Page 111*
	336	dark blue
	437	warm yellow
	731	olive

Page 112
	833	grayish yellow
	320	green
	797	blue

Page 113
	931	blue
	422	beige
	3328	red

Page 114
		cream
	932	pale blue
	367	green
	437	warm yellow
	436	gold
	356	pale red
	355	dark red
	938	dark brown

Page 115
		white
		ecru
	823	dark blue
	422	beige
	801	brown

Page 116
		white
	676	dull yellow
	407	pale brownish red
	938	dark brown
	761	pale red
	347	red
	932	pale blue
	367	green

Page 117
		ecru
	842	pale gray
	920	terra-cotta
	918	dark terra-cotta
	422	beige
	3052	pale grayish green
	938	dark brown
	922	pale terra-cotta
	729	deep yellow

Page 118
		white
	422	beige
	898	dark brown
	347	red
	931	pale blue
	930	dark blue
	502	green

Page 119
		ecru

	422	beige
	420	pale brown
	938	dark brown
	518	cold blue
	322	warm blue

Pages 120-121
	727	pale yellow
	437	warm yellow
	347	red
	367	green
	798	blue

Page 122*
		white
		ecru
	738	pale beige
	676	yellow
	436	gold
	407	pale reddish brown
	632	dark reddish brown
	223	pale claret
	347	red
		black

Page 123
		white
	644	pale gray
	640	dark gray
	676	yellow

	433	brown
	223	pale claret
	221	dark claret
		black

Page 126

	422	beige
	502	bluish green
	221	dark claret
	930	dark grayish blue

Page 127

		ecru
	422	beige
	420	pale brown
	869	brown
	938	dark brown
	931	grayish blue
	3354	pale old rose
	3350	dark old rose

Page 128

	320	green
	436	gold
	435	dark gold
	367	dark green

Page 129

		white
	437	warm yellow
	436	gold
	898	dark brown

| | 920 | terra-cotta |

Page 130

		white
	437	warm yellow
	898	dark brown
	347	red
	311	blue

Page 131

	422	beige
	347	red
	938	dark brown
		black
	367	green

Page 132

	422	beige
	842	pale gray
	938	dark brown
	926	pale greenish blue
	437	warm yellow
	3371	brownish black
	801	brown
	347	red

Page 133

		ecru
	422	beige
	644	pale gray
	221	dark claret
	470	green

	930	dark grayish blue
	938	dark brown
	931	grayish blue

Page 134

		white
	738	pale beige
	744	yellow
	422	beige
	433	brown
	347	red
	869	brown
		black

Page 135

		white
	739	pale beige
	422	beige
	420	brown
	347	red
		black

Page 136

	437	warm yellow
	300	reddish brown
	402	pale orange
	760	pale red
	830	greenish brown
	347	red

*To be sewn on red material

14

PATTERNS FROM THE BALKANS

Ida-Merete Erlandsen

The cross stitch is a small, fast stitch made by two stitches crossing each other. It is solid and wears well. One would think this little square phenomenon of a stitch has a limited usefulness. Not so — it can express itself in many ways, and it is used all over the world.

The patterns in this section are taken from the Balkans and are characteristic expressions of the different countries: Bulgarian and Rumanian patterns express joy in home and flowers of the garden, Hungarian designs are more heraldic, whereas Yugoslavian designs are tight and geometrical. The same tendency can be found in the northern part of Greece, but on the southern coast the joy of living takes over and the cross stitch work pictures boats, houses, and roosters, which are symbols of fertility.

All the patterns originate from costumes or useful objects in the home. Whether they are serious and tight or free and colorful, the patterns make a similiar use of space. The space not covered by stitches is used — just as in music — to give emphasis to the embroidered areas. It gives them character and rhythm. Also it makes the patterns easy to sew. The emphasis throughout is fresh and bold and full of fantasy so that one gets the impression they are created happily and with a great sense of the use of color. Such creation comes from a rich tradition developed through many generations and with many varied themes, in which the original naturalism has been forced into a decorative form. One can't help but stop and think how and where these patterns originated. This is why they are meaningful to us, even though they come from different countries. They are "timeless" as well as "placeless".

Maybe we don't embroider colorful borders on the sleeves of our husbands' shirts, but we can find many other uses for these stitches in our daily lives.

The Balkans

16

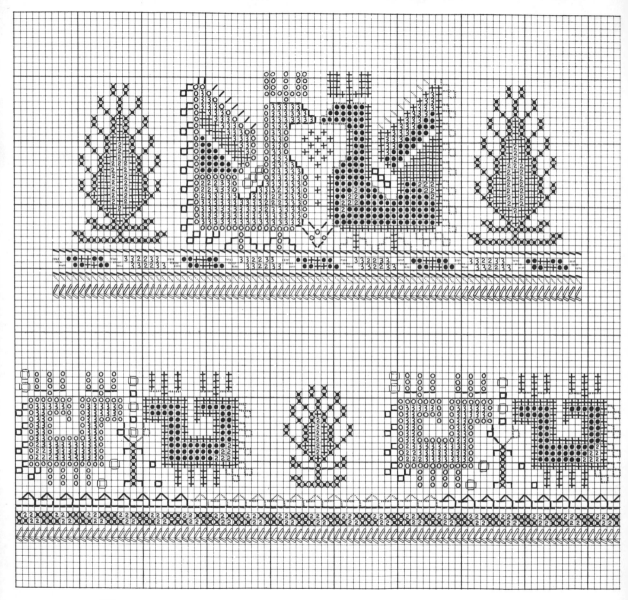

18

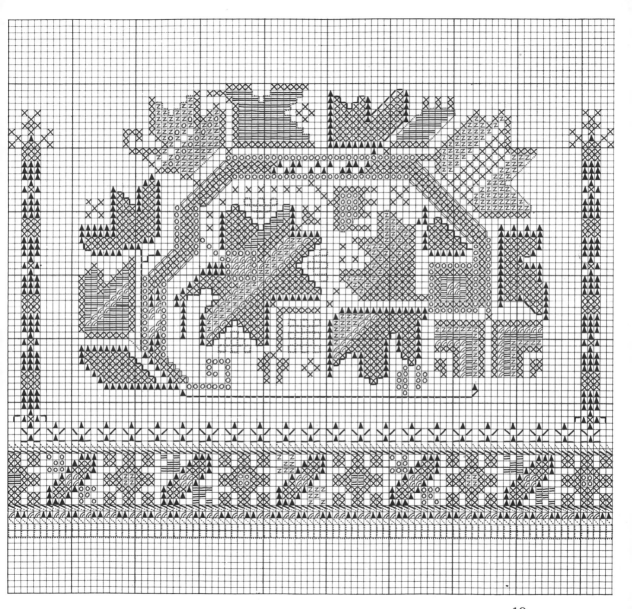

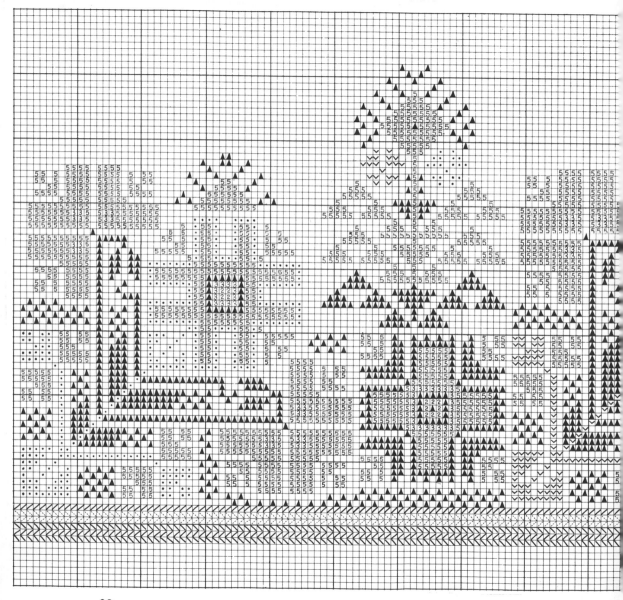

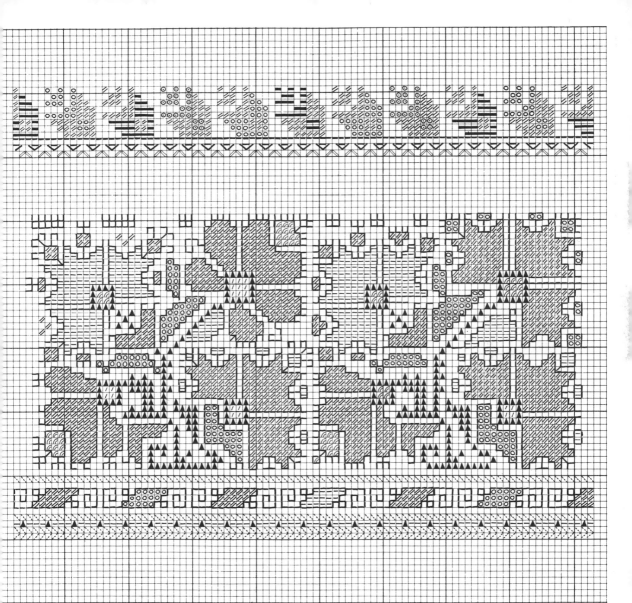

23

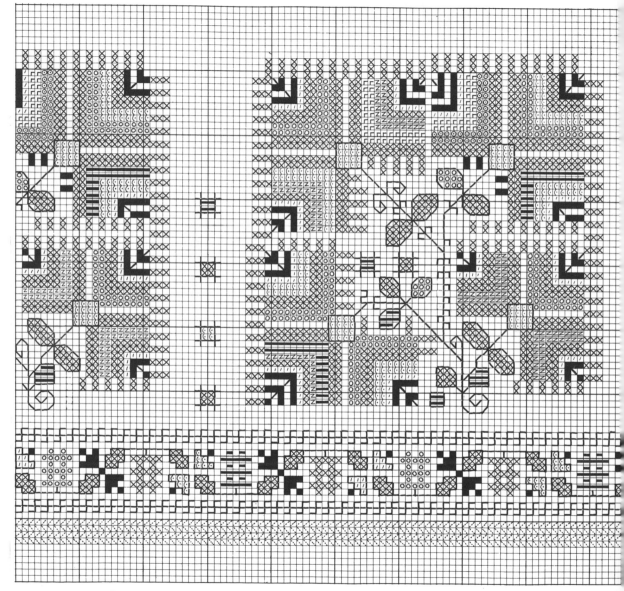

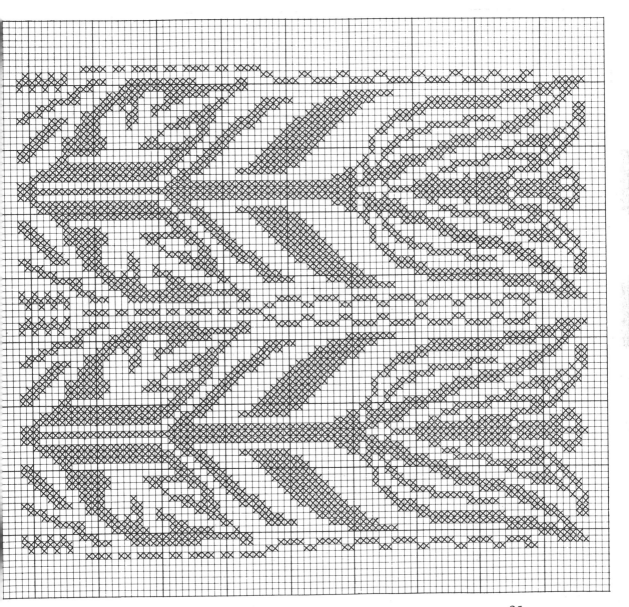

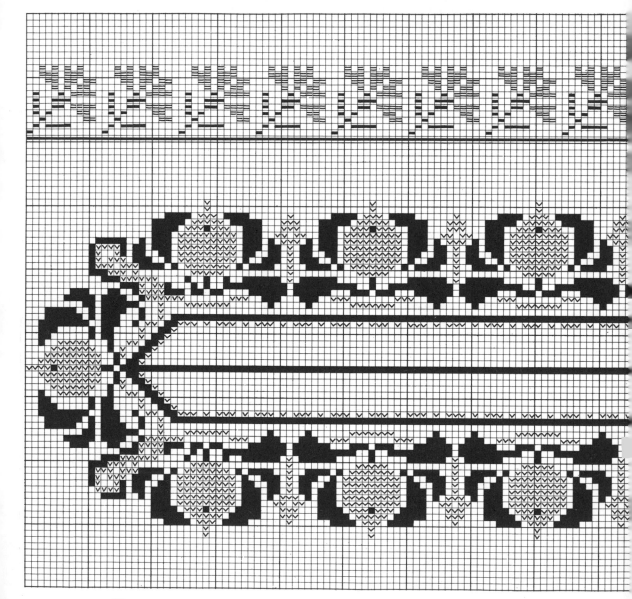

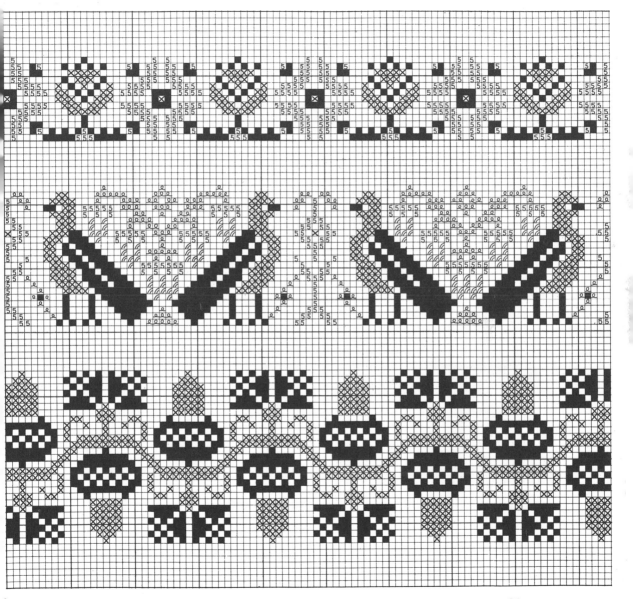

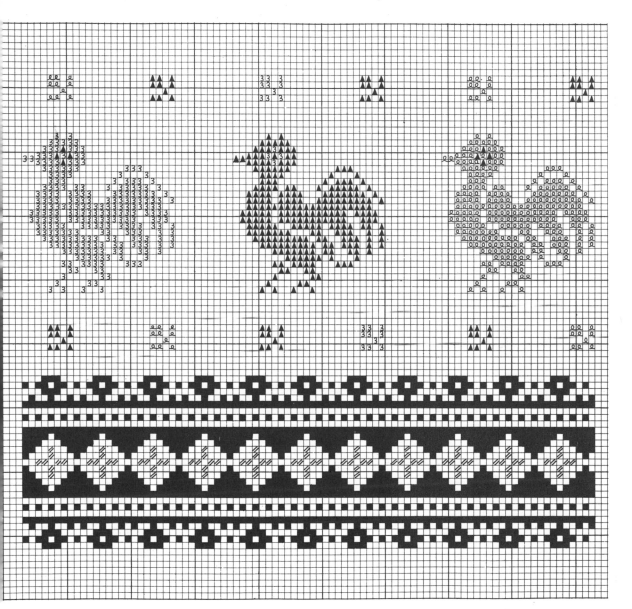

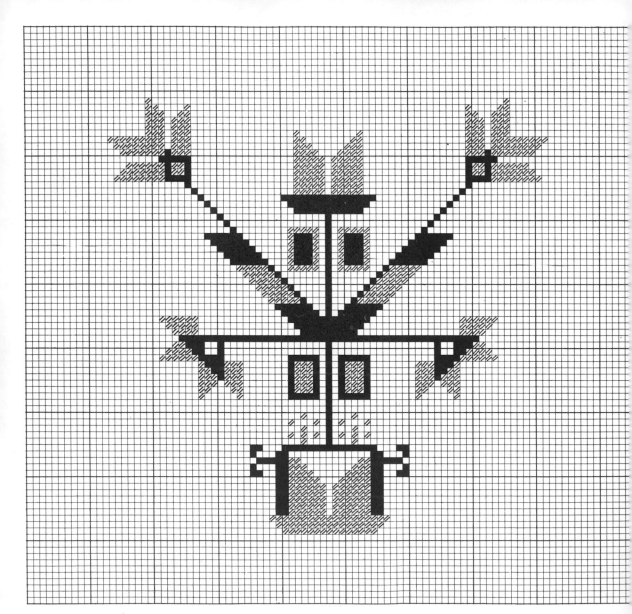

34

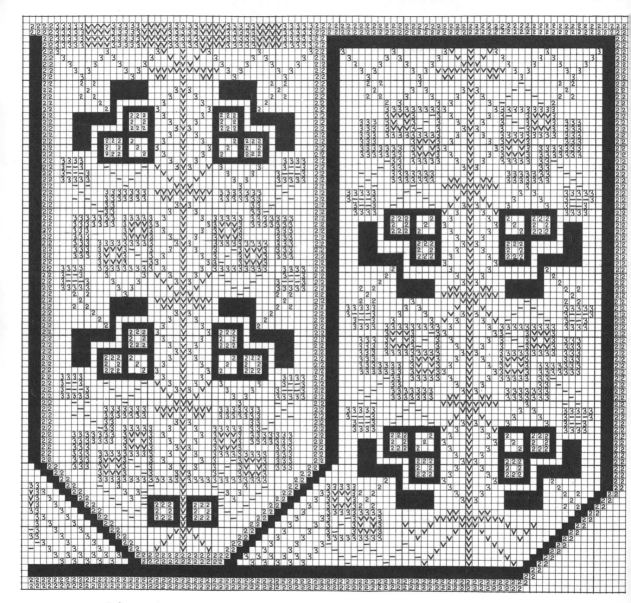

36

37

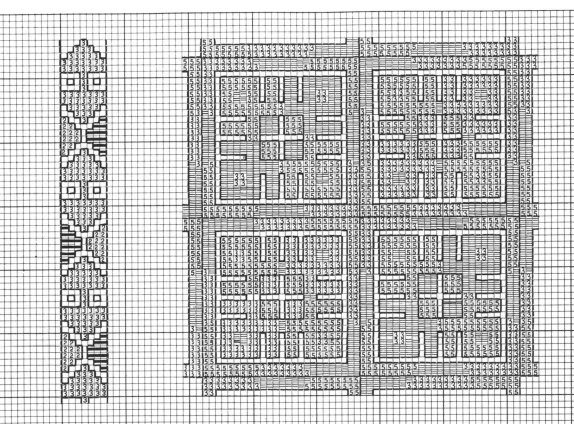

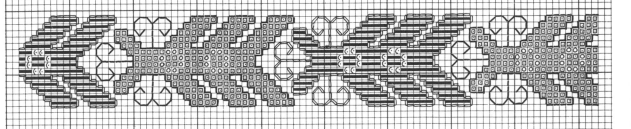

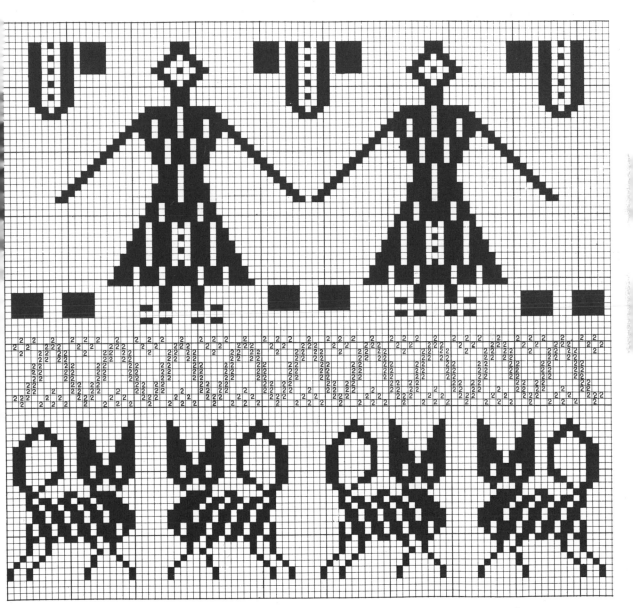

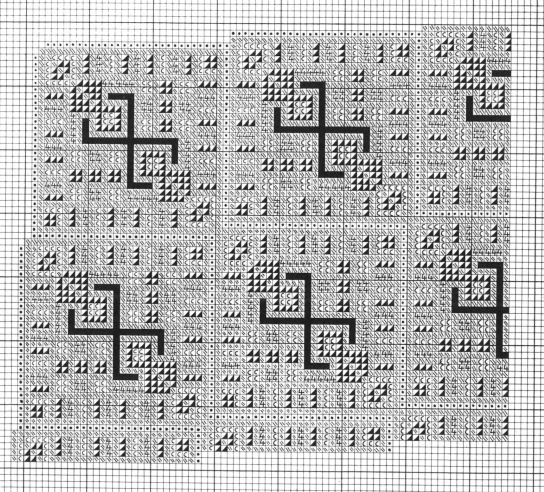

42

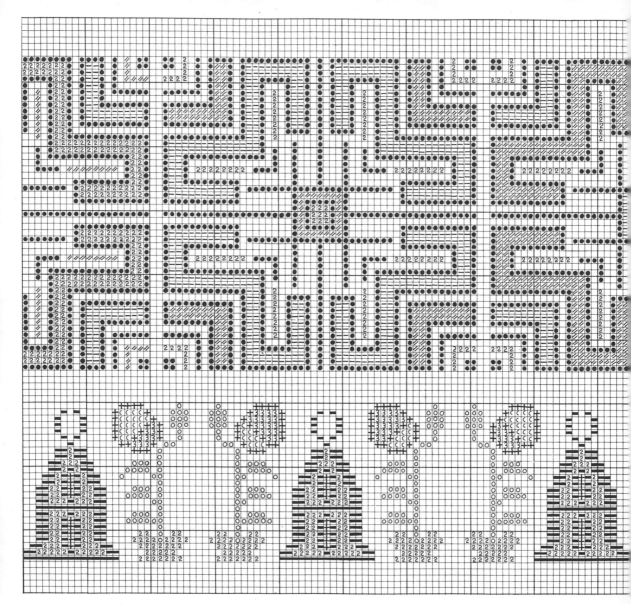

44

46

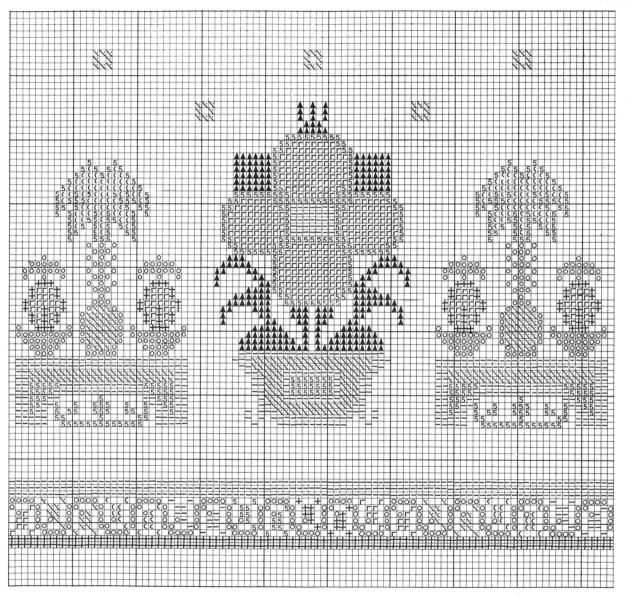

48

PATTERNS FROM ANCIENT CHINA

Antonette Prip-Møller

In publishing once more (after an interval of many years and because of many requests) a collection of old Chinese cross stitch patterns, I send my grateful thoughts to those women of China who, particularly during the period of our travels round the country in 1929-1933, helped me collect old items of handwork. For the most part these originate from the inland provinces of China and have been used as bed curtains, pillows, sleeve borders, children's aprons, and ankle-bands.

"Say it with symbols" applies to a very great extent to the examples of folk embroidery we shall concern ourselves with in this chapter. The motifs of the patterns have been taken from many sources — from religion, the animal and plant worlds — and express wishes for good luck, long life, riches and many sons, happiness, important offices, etc. They represented the ordinary peasant woman's way of decorating cotton garments, gifts to friends, trousseaux, wedding presents, etc. All the good wishes were thus worked into the patterns, the object being that the person who wore the garments or used the pillow or the child provided with the apron would benefit accordingly.

As a rule, the patterns were embroidered with white hand-twisted cotton thread on blue cotton homespun, or with blue stitches on white material; but several colors were sometimes used too. Some of the common symbols are:

lotus flower—holy Buddhist symbol of purity
peony—riches
gourd, pomegranate—fertility
phoenix—the Empress
dragon—the Emperor
bat—happiness
heron—longevity
fish—many children, endurance, alertness
butterfly, cherryblossom, peach-blossom—new life, happiness, beauty
coins—riches
endless knot (group of stacked boxes), swastika—infinity, long life

My interest in folk embroidery has always been stimulated in particular by the thought of the diligent peasant woman who, with small means, yet rich in imagination and expectation, embroidered her thoughts, feelings, and dreams into these simple items of handcraft. I remember a trip down the Yangtze River when we came to a flooded area. I caught sight of a woman sitting in a doorway on shore, embroidering. The water was lapping at her clay house, but she kept on at her work, presumably hoping the water would not reach her little home — perhaps she was embroidering good luck symbols on a child's apron.

You will find small irregularities on the patterns and perhaps think they must be drawing errors. But you will often discover that they serve instead to soften the pattern and make it even lovlier. The corners are thus often different — you may either follow the patterns of the originals as in the book or make your own corners.

It is my hope that this book will provide pleasure for those who enjoy needlework, and that many beautiful things will result from these patterns — which may be combined at will and embroidered in whatever colors seem most suitable.

51

52

53

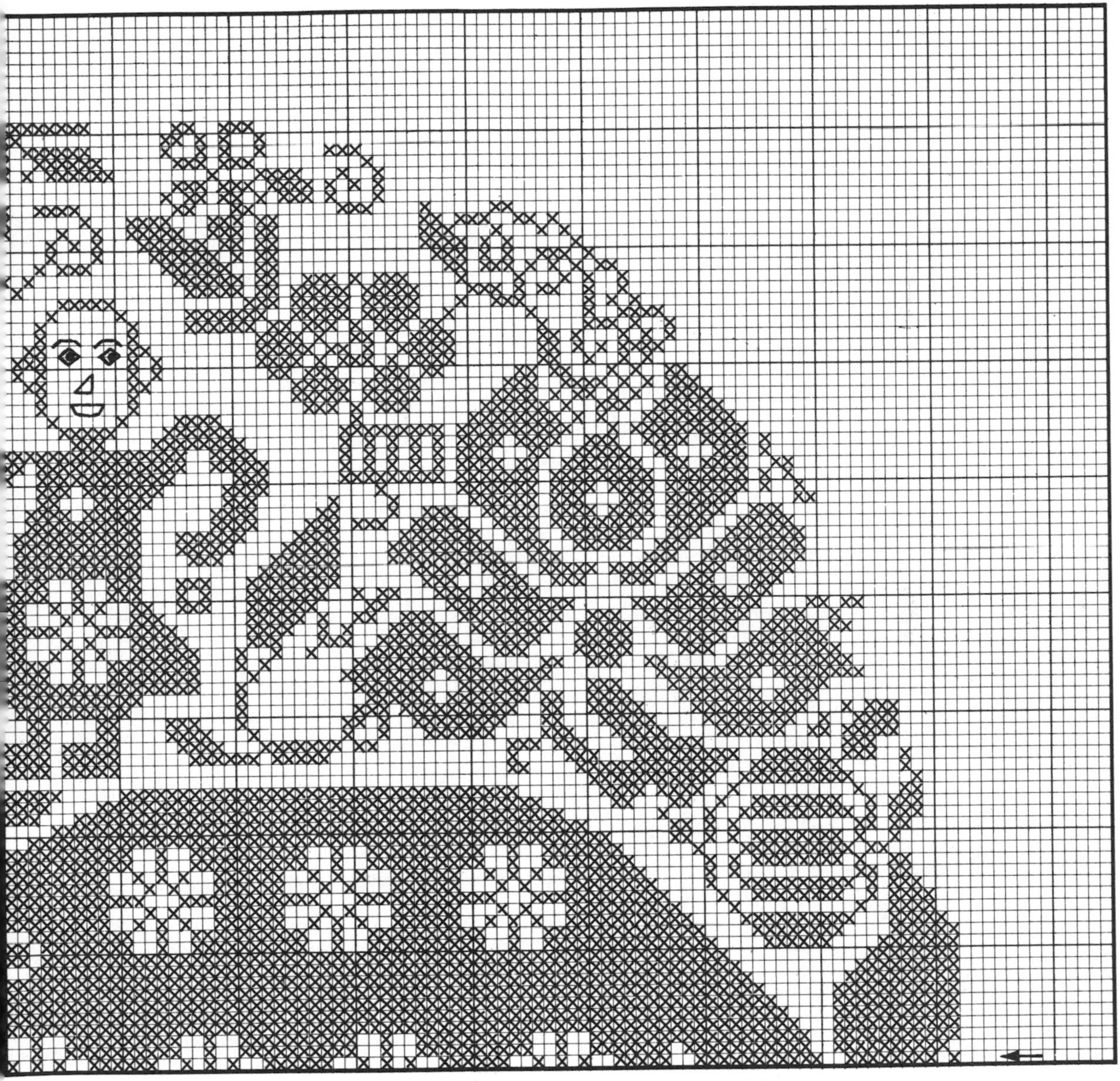

See also 58 and 59

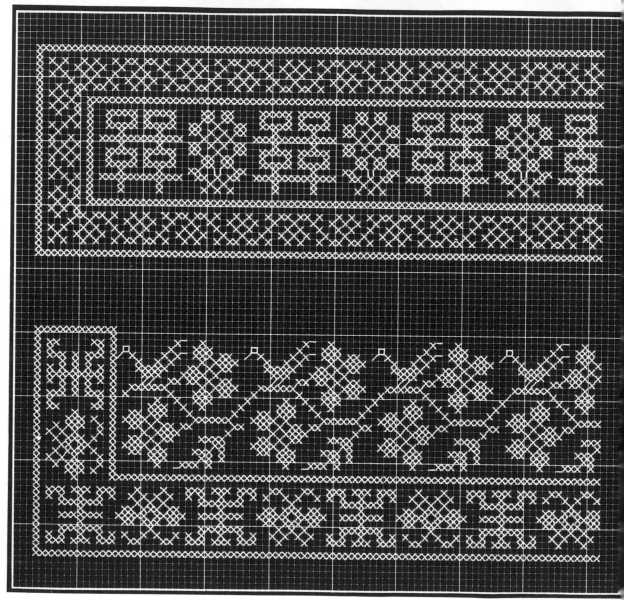

See also 64 and 65

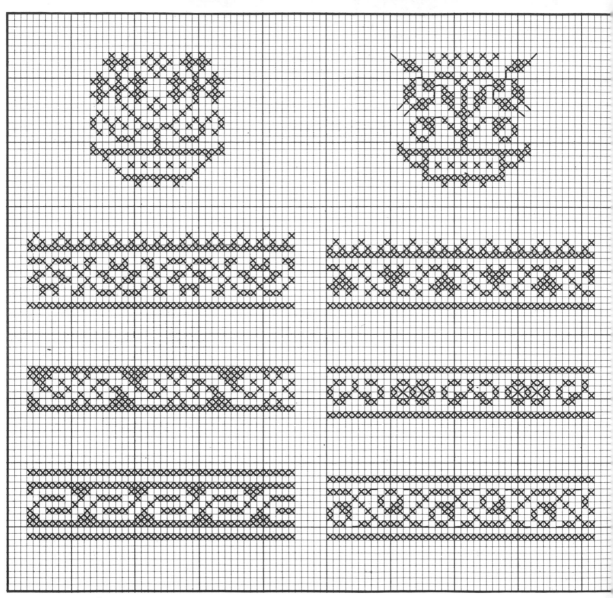

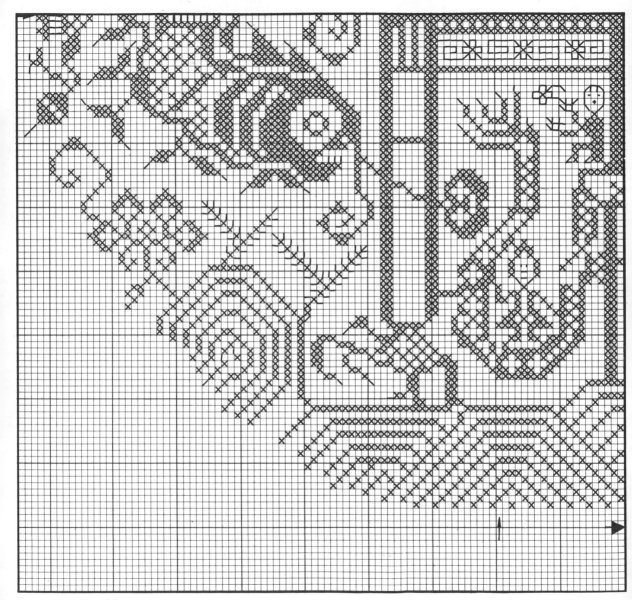

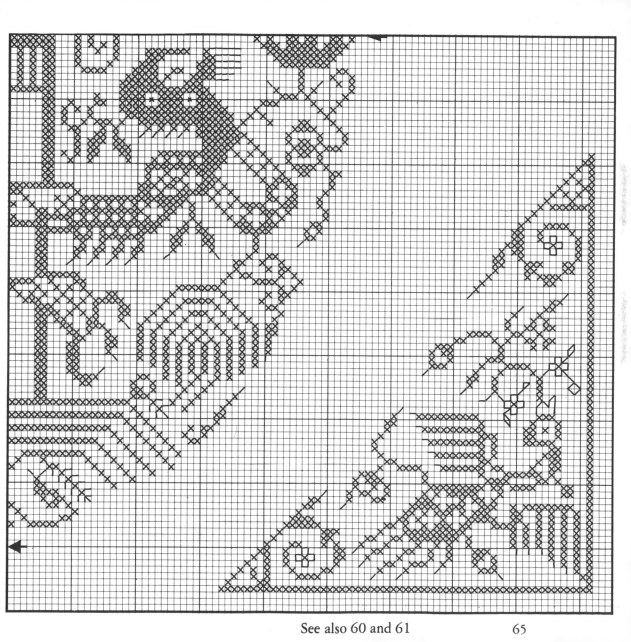

See also 60 and 61

See also 74 and 75

72

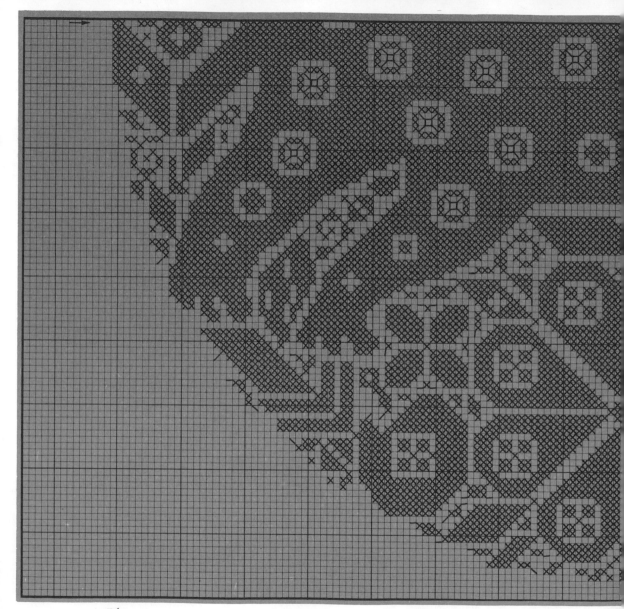

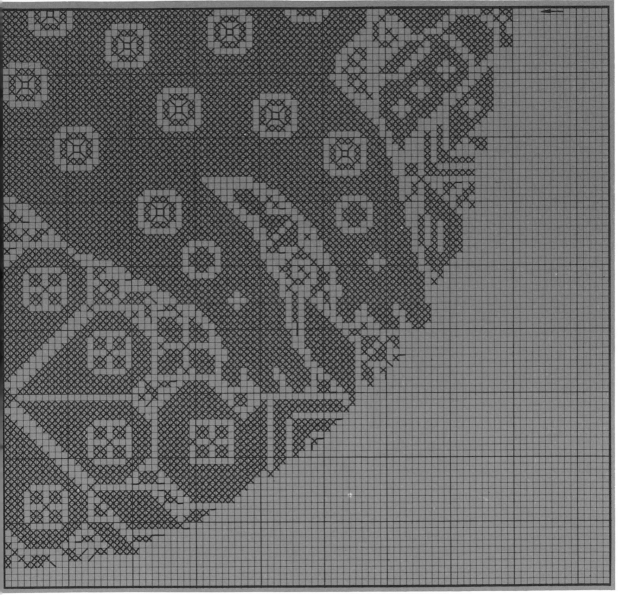

See also 70 and 71

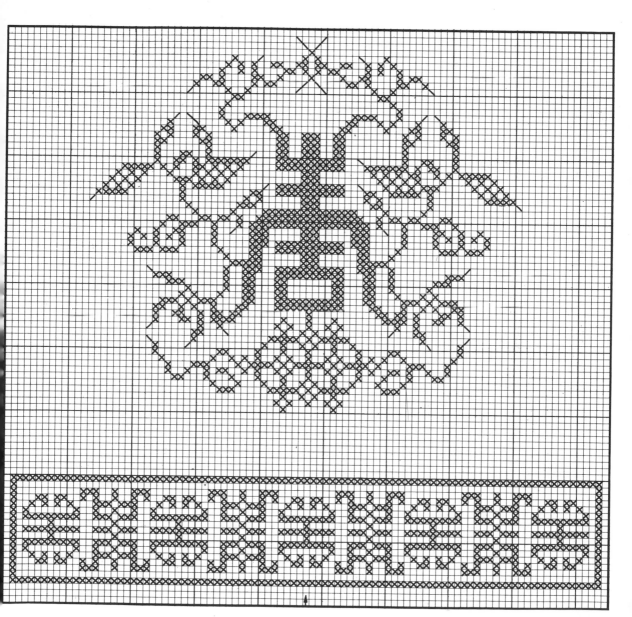

70

81

PATTERNS FROM DENMARK

Else Johnsen

In the old needlecraft many figures are repeated in an infinite number of variations. The reason for the repetition is that these figures were originally thought of as symbols and were only sewn as such. For example, a ship and a stately building were symbols of the church, whereas a tree was the tree of life. Wreaths signified eternity or eternal friendship, and they were almost always used to frame samplers.

Later on, when patterns were used purely decoratively, many figures from daily life were added. One can almost imagine how a wife or girl working on her sampler suddenly noticed a blackbird, chicken, goose, or even a dog in the yard and decided to incorporate it into her design. After all, the great fun of working in cross stitch is that, even though cross stitch is a tight technique, it is possible to depict animals with only a few stitches. In the early, primitive needlecraft one can find people in the designs. On a sampler from Graested done in 1820 the decorative falconer shown on page 84 was found. He is from the period in which needlecraft design developed from the naive to an unfortunately naturalistic expression. It is certainly no surprise that I found a great many samplers with boat motifs in a fishing village. The patterns, adapted from older samplers, were undoubtedly chosen because the women's husbands or fiances were sailors or fishermen. As in most cross stitch work, these figures are pure fairytale ships. They have storage extensions, flags, and pennants but they are always primarily decorative, and after they were framed they must have enlivened the small rooms where they usually hung. A number of the patterns are taken from bed linens, which were always in red or blue. On samplers, however, the patterns were sewn in many colors. I hope you will find these old patterns both amusing and decorative. They offer unlimited possibilities for use.

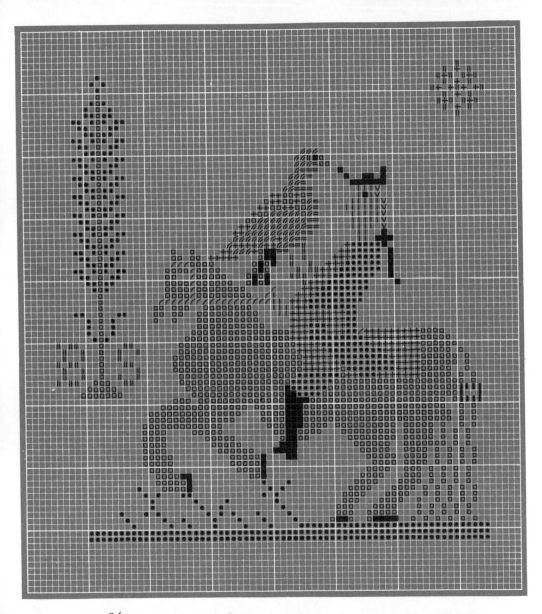

85

PATTERNS FROM ANCIENT PERU

Ellen Jessen

At one time it was thought that the whole of the rich culture already in existence in Peru when the Europeans arrived was created by the Incas. However, the fabrics that have made Peruvian textiles famous originated from the culture that flourished in the 2000 years preceding the Spanish conquest of Peru in 1532. The reason why so many old textiles were to be found in Peru in a good state of preservation is that the Peruvians gave their dead rich burial presents and in many of the tombs in the dry coastal desert sands the materials have kept well. The cultures best known for their textiles are: *Paracas,* during the first centuries of the Christian Era; *Tiahuanaco,* about the end of the first millenium; and *Inca,* during the hundred years immediately preceding the Spanish conquest.

Paracas. These patterns can be divided into two groups, the geometrical and the naturalistic. The geometrical patterns are built up of embroidered straight lines on a plain background. The colors are most frequently red (background), green or olive, dark blue, and warm yellow. Figures are outlined alternately in one color and then the next, until finally the pattern color sequence repeats itself. The inner lines will often repeat the figure in a new way (frequently upside down). As a rule, the figures are stylized and fantastic with, for example, a head at either end, and one figure is often entwined in the next.

The naturalistic figures are composed of rounded outlines completely filled in with stem stitch. Sometimes they are quite true to life and consist of only a few colors but more frequently they are multicolored and composed of characteristics of various living beings, who may wear masks and carry belongings.

Tiahuanaco. Tiahuanaco, now in Bolivia, was in ancient times a religious center. Most of the characteristic motifs of the fine tapestries of this style are also to be found in the Sun Gate, a large relief monument there. In addition to straight lines, right angles, small animal heads, and head gear, there are repeated motifs of a mouth with carnivorous teeth, a weeping winged eye, and an eye divided into light and dark halves by a straight line. On the ponchos there is often what appears to be a completely abstract pattern in broad, vertical borders. Each border is divided up into smaller units by means of vertical, horizontal, and sloping zig-zag lines, each containing a motif. There are usually two motifs in each border but, as in the case of the Paracas embroideries, they have been employed many times over — partly by turning them in different directions, and partly by using two or three colors arranged according to a definite system. The colors are usually yellow, orange, and light brown, with a limited use of blue, green, and light and dark reds.

Inca. The Inca textiles are distinguished by their exquisite techniques rather than by their great fantasy. The patterns are usually composed of small squares with various figures that are often geometrical. The best known textiles are finely woven ponchos in tapestry weaving. Often they have a V-shaped section surrounding the head slit, in which the pattern stands out in contrast to the remainder.

On the plates, cross stitch, staggered cross stitch, and stem stitch have been used. In general, Paracas motifs can be found on the first plates, Tiahuanaco motifs on the middle plates, and Inca motifs on the final plates.

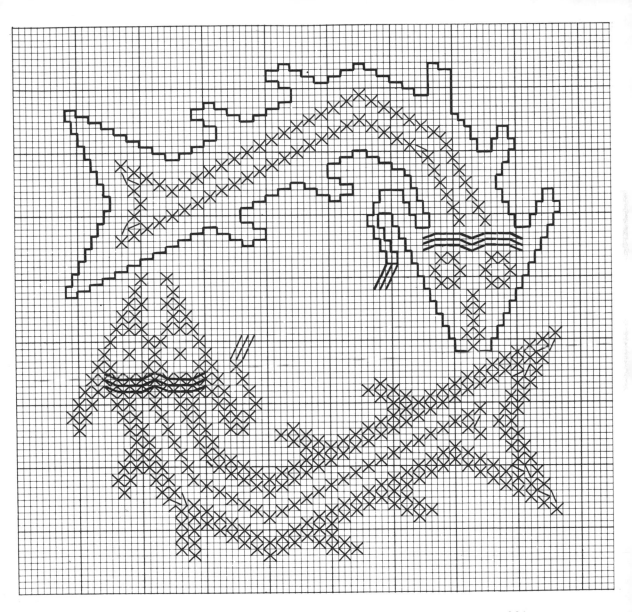

101

102

103

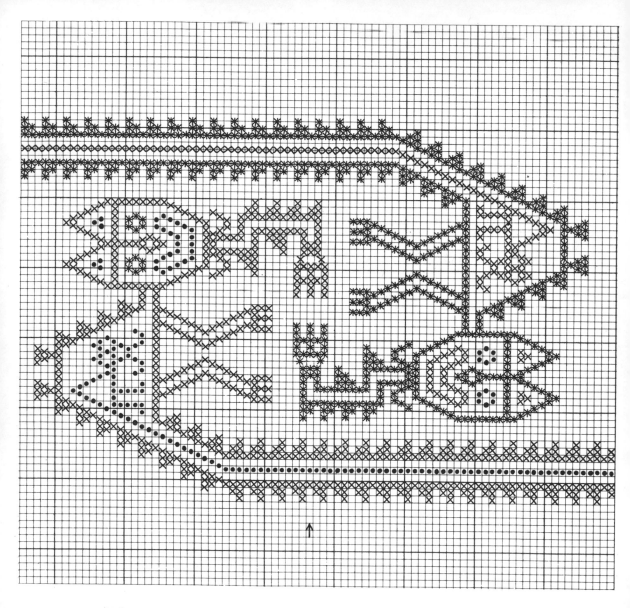

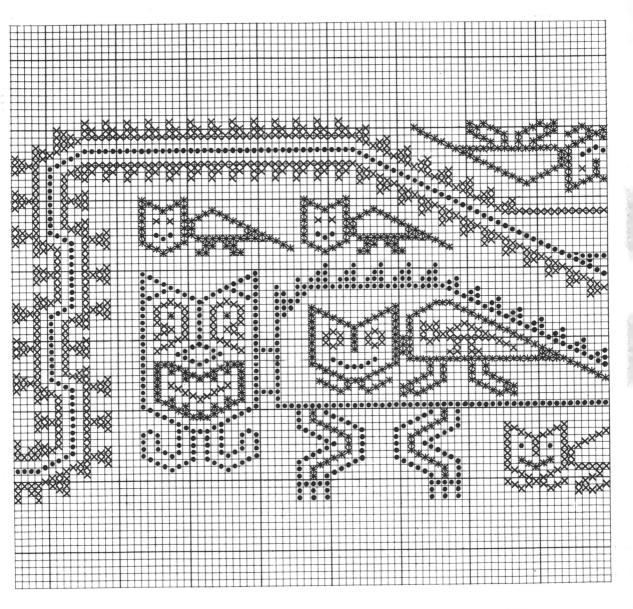

105

106

107

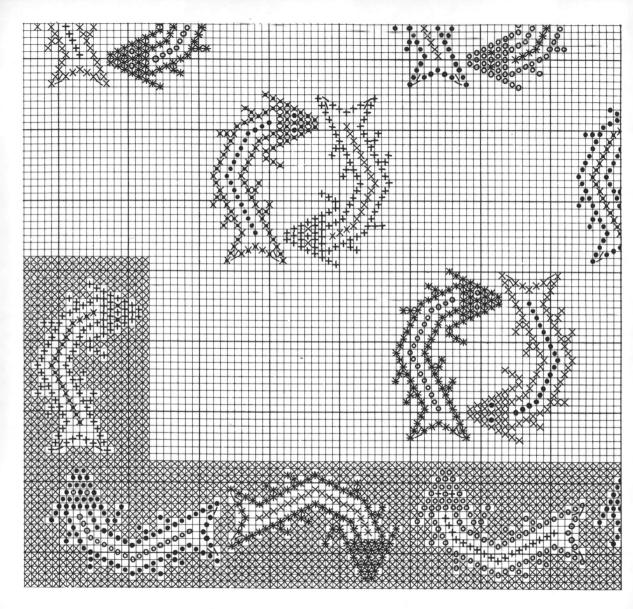

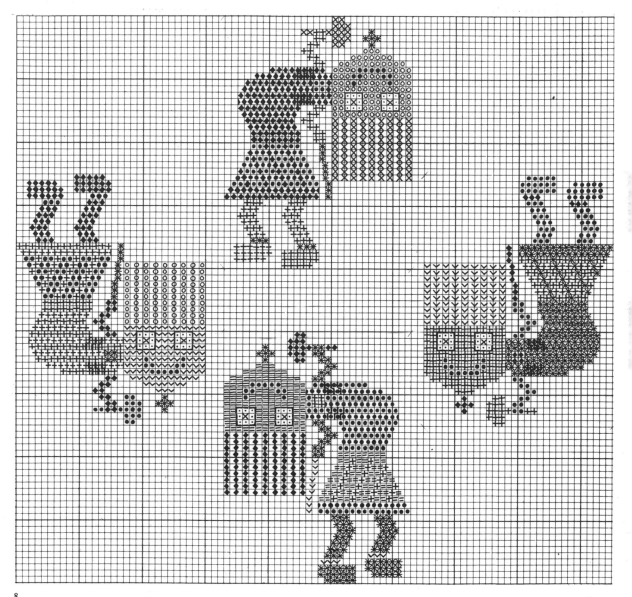

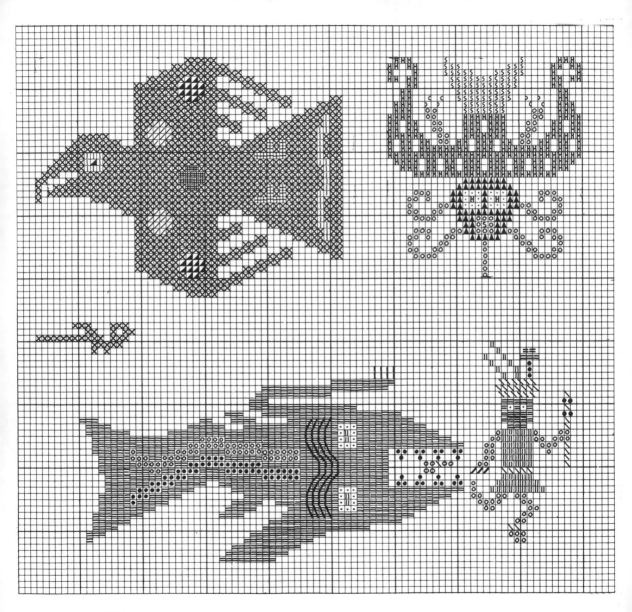

110

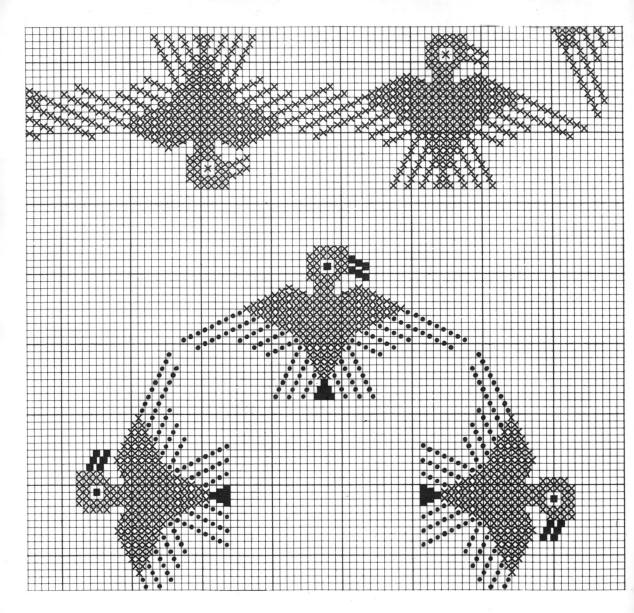

112

114

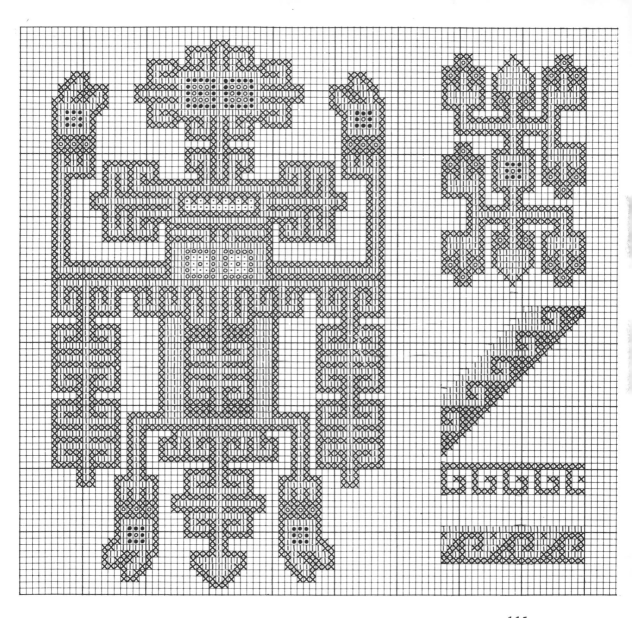

115

116

117

118

119

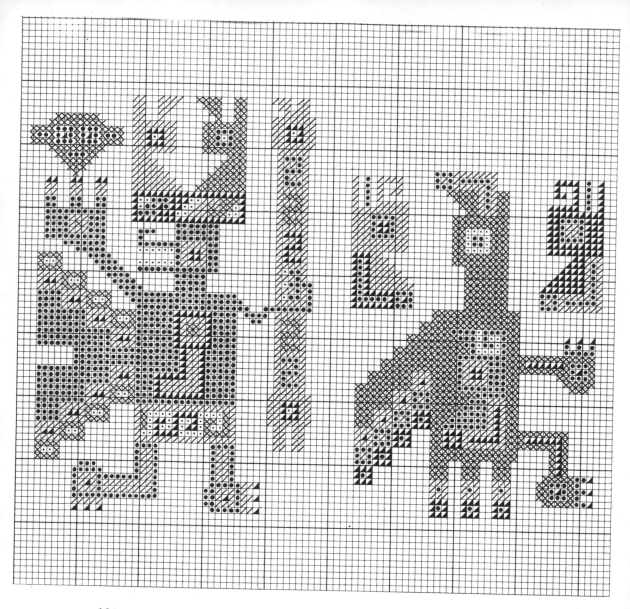

120

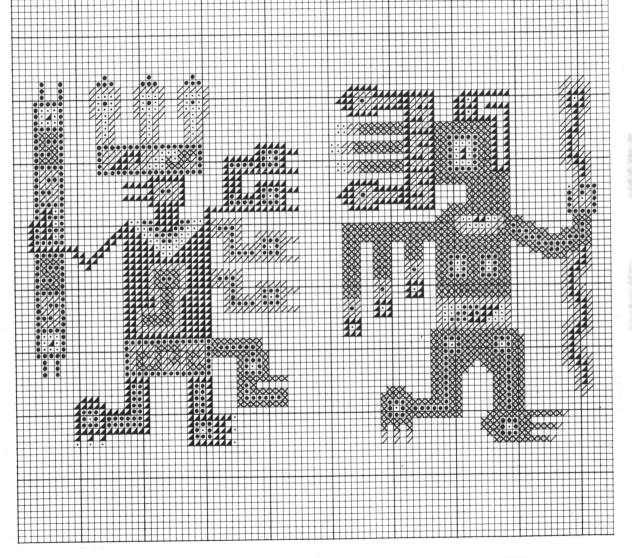

121

122

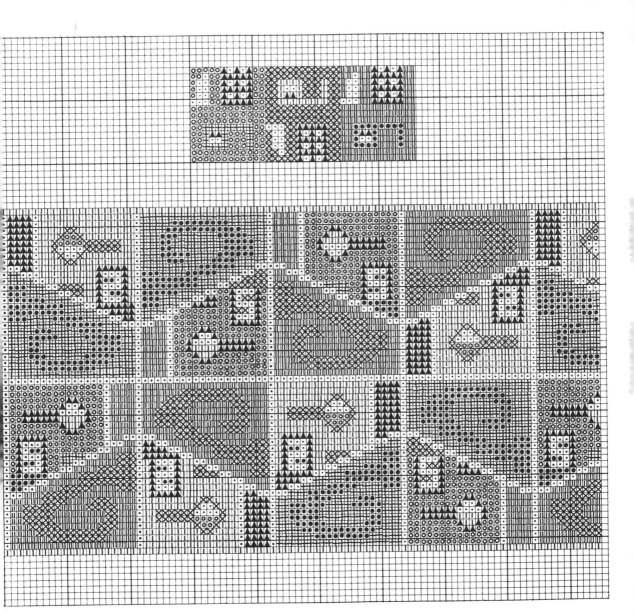

123

124

9

126

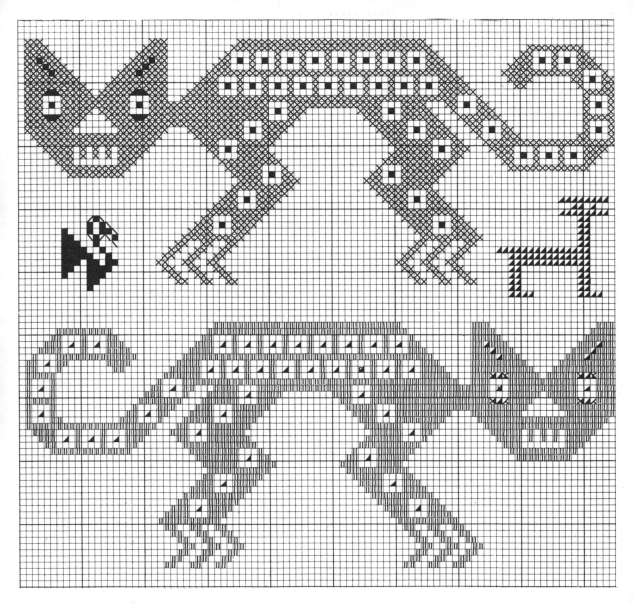

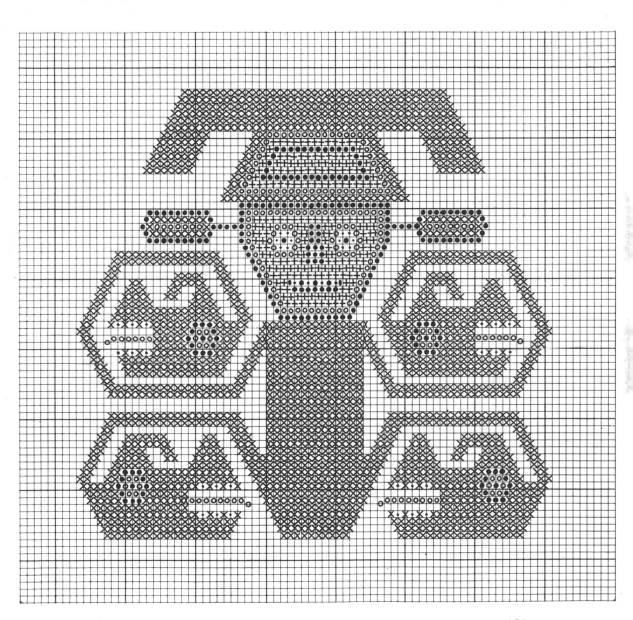

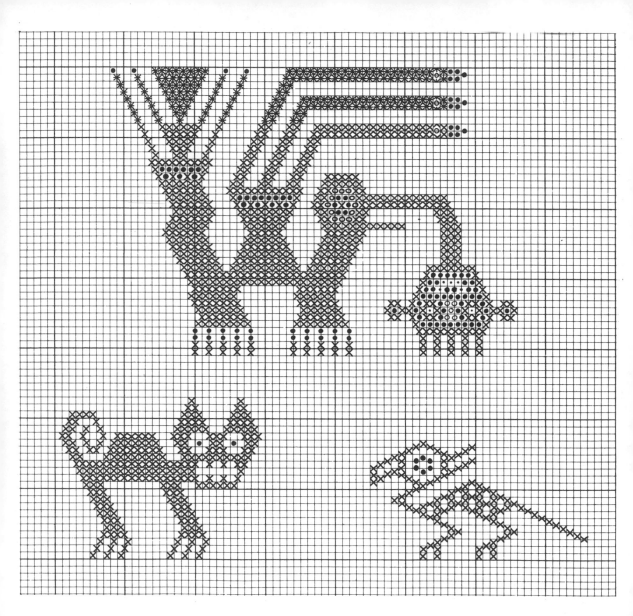

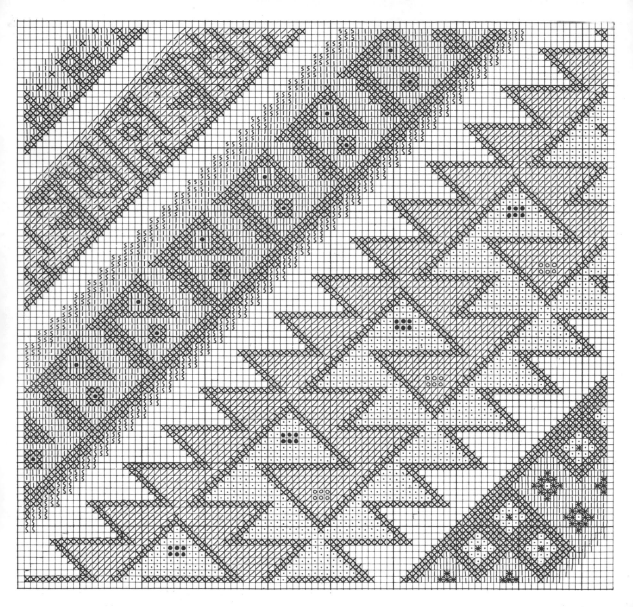

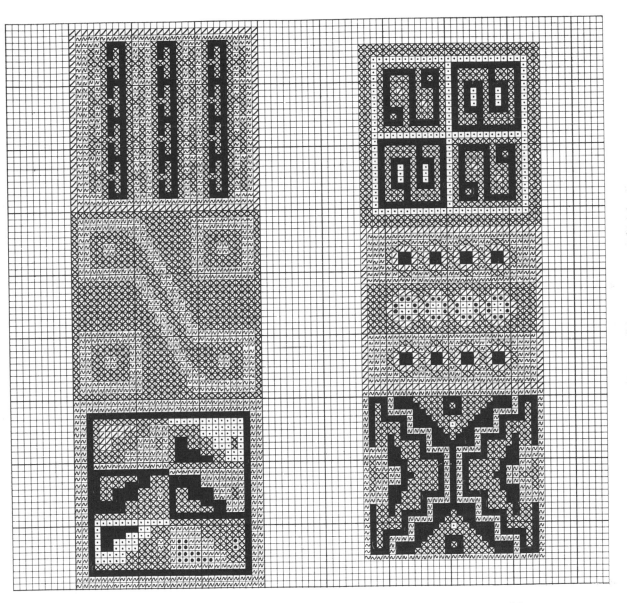

135

136